WHY IS MY HEART IN MY THROAT?

J. TRAFFORD

TRAFFORD
ESTATE

Copyright © 2026 by J. Trafford
All rights reserved. No part of this book may be reproduced in any manner whatsoever without written permission except in the case of brief quotations embodied in critical articles and reviews.
First Edition, Paperback Edition 2026

Cover artwork by Katrina Kaufman.
Photography by J. Power.

INTRODUCTION BY MEGHA PAI

"Vulture"

You roamed the city with a pack of matches, burning everything you deemed wasn't *fine art*, letting flames lick the sides of the bridges you so detested, metal beams falling through the windows of skyscrapers, punching out the glass—your laugh blended with the cackling of vultures as they swooped down from the rafters & pecked among wreckage for a stray eyeball, a lonely tendon, as you surveyed the destruction & thought *yes, this is my element*—

Dear Readers, Listeners and Empty Dreamers:

I first met J. Trafford when we started college in 2009. During that first week of school, freshmen were given their choice of potential field trips—excursions like going to a football game, visiting a local amusement park, and spending the day at a renaissance fair. Of course, we both chose the renaissance fair.

J. introduced me to The Smiths (beyond the well-known "How Soon Is Now?") and rallied our friends into spontaneous graveyard walks. He'd workshop his song lyrics in poetry class, ask you to perform with his band (recognizing that you had the vocal chops you didn't realize you had), lend an ear when you felt depressed, and encourage you to share your own art—even when you were filled with self-doubt.

Although J.'s bands and projects have evolved over the years, his unique artistic vision has carried through his works. Whether you're listening to Suavity's Mouthpiece, Sommelier, Nowhere Wolves, or J. Trafford solo, you'll experience that vision for yourself.

As I look back on our 16 years of friendship, I'm thankful to have learned and grown alongside a sharp, funny and supportive artist like J. At the root of it, that's what creating art's all about: self-expression received by supportive friends and a broader community of creatives lifting each other up —especially during times like these.

And if you make something that you deem isn't *fine art*, don't be afraid to burn it down and start again. I know I have.

Megha Pai
Writer and Comedian

WHY IS MY HEART IN MY THROAT?

"Empty Dreamer"
2002: Non-album single

>Who knows me better than you?
>A single man, father of two
>Would I commit this murder?
>Aimless in a secondhand store
>
>I've finally decided not to care anymore
>Empty nest; empty dreamer.
>
>The people were astounded
>at your picture in the paper
>"What a pity, such a dashing individual
>turned to a life of hard crime!"
>Careless in a secondhand store
>
>I've finally decided not to live anymore
>Empty nest; empty dreamer.
>
>The suspect's lover is in tears
>The boy she loves, everyone fears
>And yet, just the other night
>they had explored the politics of young love -
>he'd let her down again...
>
>The people scream, "He's on the run!"
>"Let's protect human life!"

They exclaim, grabbing guns
Lifeless in a worthwhile war

I've just decided
not to write or sing anymore
I just let you down again.
But I couldn't help myself
How do you expect me to help you?

"Rejected By the Denied"
2005: *The Winedark Serenatas*

Trace with your eyes,
the clement vines gently climb the abbey walls
With a time world-weary
and soft I kiss into your turning tresses

I cannot forgive, and I cannot forget!
You'll find me lurking where archangels reign
On the amber esplanade.

Dangling from the steeple,
to again the horror of the onlooking people
O, the glamor of evil!

I cannot forgive, and I cannot forget.

"'Twixt the Landmines Glissade We"
2005: *The Winedark Serenatas*

    'Twixt the landmines glissade we
    To beneath the blooming hemlock
    Intoxicated with the boldest of liquors: love
    I drop to my knees on the wet grass and leaves,
    but swinging back, you're no longer behind me.
    Dying buds in curls and locks,
    smoldering ash blue skies retreat

    'Twixt the burning beams glissade I
    To beneath the kneading, bleeding oak
    Intoxicated with the thickest liquor
    (caught in the Wheel of Life's spokes.)

    Among the orchids we spent eternity
    'til the day the bombs bloomed consuming you and me
    When the judge asked you winsomely declared
    My angel could not have killed these three
    O, but dearest the day will come
    when you'll see the horror that is the true me!
    Yes, and dearest when that day comes
    What will you have left to do but run?

"The Estate"
2005: *The Winedark Serenatas*

    At the pinnacle
    of your conception
    Genetics interlaced philharmonically
    with the science of Heaven.

    My family's manor estate burned down today
    I tried - but the scorching stock certificates
    could not be saved.

    I have not yet found God, but the sinners have found me.

"I Know in My Heart"
2006: *Embrace the Nocturne*

>What has been done, has been done
>I am not proud
>(at least...not aloud.)
>
>In my heart I know
>I am not at fault
>No sin tarnishes
>the silver lining of conscience
>
>We are the last of our kind left on the planet
>There is no right, this is all wrong
>O, nature forgive me!
>Such ample sod, a fertile son screams
>"NO!"
>
>In my heart, I know
>what has been done
>can never be undone.

"The Day Dawns Slowly"
2006: *Embrace the Nocturne*

>Azure heart, viridescent heart
>Breach me
>Make me sonorous with Nature's art:

Then it is day,
the solicitude soothes my senses.

Infinite maelstrom
counter to the ebb of which
you will not endure.

Don't waste your breath
for I do not love, nor could I ever
one so simple and homely as you!

Here the matter ends
here my senses transcend

"And Ardor Nevermore"
2006: *Embrace the Nocturne*

> Draw the nightshades on worn, forgotten skies
> Tonight will not be your night!
>
> Pinch me, I must be dreaming
> for you have yet to break our moonlit embrace,
> but what I feel, and who I am
> is inescapable.
>
> Sweet sixteen and never been whisked.

"Killjoy"
2008: *Citta Creatura Viva*

> The bottle that you so hopefully twirl
> slows to a spinning stop neck facing me, and
> how all your innermost wants and dreams
> erupt in an allegorical spring
>
> Your once proudly-held shoulders drop
> your damp eyes, too, fall.
> And with a sympathetic pat, your friends assure you,
> "It's just one little kiss, that's all."
>
> ...as you toss yourself from the overpass
> My first kiss was your last.

"Celeste"
2008: *Citta Creatura Viva*

> I was there, a gargoyle rapt up in the rafters
> as delirium spat you out into the world
> O child of the stern, earthen floorwork
> paled blue by the fire in the hearth
> To assure that the rest of existence
> would perish in discordant chaos
> Upon the shutting of your sacred opal eyes.
>
> But to mother, dear mother, those eyes were crude
> and lidded from the handicap. And one Sisyphean night
> she biked up the cobblestone paved bridge.
>
> I was there, you grew, and through
> years of extended stares and muffled whispers
> You soon knew those piggish other children
> were making fun of you.
>
> And you cursed the God that I serve,
> and who made you clearly in image,
> but never in likeness.
>
> Can you feel the aurora now?
> My hand grips around your throat?
> An angel avenged.

"Know Your Place"
2009: The Audial Equivalent of John Wilkes Booth

And I must ask you: Is this not what you meant
by living a life in shambles?
Well, I couldn't have asked for anything more.

Kenneth Branagh shuts his eyes
- this is the worst display of poetry he's ever known
But this song keeps my Rolls gassed and
pinning John Mayer's bones.

Honest Abe slouches, slumped over
his seat - I'll tell you the truth
I'm the audial equivalent to John Wilkes Booth.

See clearly, the window /
Once we were pretty as prom queens,
As I lie on the curling blades of grass /
but make no mistake
Read my lips, kiss each page /
Your luggage will be impounded if left
Lay softly your head on the glass /
unattended at JFK

We wrecked, smug, and rotten souls
are closing in on Radio City!

"King of Love"
2009: *I Call it Madness, But You Call it Love*

> Under duress
> he lingers on French steps
> and no sound tattoos the ever perfect quiet
>
> Houselights fade in the oh-so salient night
> Inside lovers' hearts make room for curiosity seething
> with no clue or care who's in the street.
>
> As if someone would even know his name
> If they knew who he was, they would not
> treat him such ways
> History will bury his fate.

"The Brains of Flies"
2010: *The Passion of Suavity's Mouthpiece*

> The blood is dry on the subject,
> nothing can ever be done
> All that could be writ has been writ
> dealing with the wild weirdness of our sins
> We've tripped and scraped our shins
> and mother, the blood is dry now
>
> Your spit and my spit become
> one and the same

Reeling around R.E.M., all of my minds
peruse several schools of love,
all at once from petal to stem
I could have very easily lived without the
Mona Lisa.

If you leave them alone,
they will hit close to home in return
the truth hurts
in spurts
If you leave them alone
they will leave you alone in return,
and then you'll be BORED.

"Let Grief Begin With Me"
2010: *The Passion of Suavity's Mouthpiece*

Psyches slave away
as each day trudges itself into an early grave
Life's about to get a great deal more boring,
but if you let me drape my vocal cords
all around your flesh in a modus operandi
seeming heaven sent

Let grief begin with me
I say with much aplomb to mommy
as I jump out of the frying pan
into a warm, wet ennui.

With an ocean of air
flooding each lung
and each symptom looking out for
number one.

...those lost in love find it HELL
to explain themselves with anything else
than the "lyrics" to top-ten singles.

Let grief begin with me
I spit to each one of these
My phlegm scores and landscapes
the land of milk and honey.

"Lullaby"
2011: *Suavity's Mouthpiece vs. Music*

    Before you are a dream,
    I sing of you that when you come to be
    you might dream...
    The world can't wait to see your face,
    and when you wake one day
    the world will be at peace
    from the joy your laughter brings.

    We will keep the darkness away
    while in quiet stillness you lay
    You are our endless joy / You are our whole wide world
    our little boy / our little girl

    So while you dream,
    dream of many wondrous things...
    The world can't wait to see your face,
    and when you wake this day
    the world will be at peace
    from the warmth your smile brings...

"Let's Get Ostracized"
2011: *The ATTACK.silence*

    I don't even wanna look in the mirror at my own eyes
    for they are too bloodshot to see

I've been in this fucking club all night,
and I ain't got the pull to dance with a single thing.

LET'S GET OSTRACIZED.
- peel away from a common thought
- completely forgot that I exist
- change love
...guess we'll find out.

One day, I will find myself
the last man on Earth
sighing at the immaculate calm.

Now, lower yourself down
onto a firm
understanding.

With thoughts like these, who needs
the Human condition?

"Charisma"
2012: *The Nuance of Suavity's Mouthpiece*

> They tell me,
> I've got moxie
> ...I'm just giving the pills something to do
> (These vibrations move animals)
> We all have these parts -
> why not put them to good use?
>
> Every day is a good hair day
> when you're me, but you never are
> so it never is.
> And when, at last, this cup I pass
> This charm will be the death of me.
>
> Paleontologists will gaze upon
> the found artifact of my bones and declare:
> MEDOCRITY SKIPPED AN AGE WITH THIS LINK
> from cultural to culture it translates
> no pleasure is guilty
> as layers of lobe burn and sing.
>
> John, I'm only printing receipts
> I can't claim to be that much more of a number
> than I'd gladly admit,
> maybe this is God's way of saying
> -BUSY SIGNAL-

I'm a pound sign, baby
I refuse to remain cool under pressure
Where's the hypocrisy
What.
Idiosyncrasy.

"Vignette"
2012: Unreleased

All the bastards!
It goes against some scientific truth
that I come to be
The opposite of a heartbeat (less and less gravity)

I must let no person into
this world, no insipid strand which
would compromise the opacity of my sight

So, I'm the villain, I'm the one to be reviled

From a bizarre misery, I survey my newfound powers:
to stop oncoming cars by stepping into the street
to add shade to the outskirts of hope in a conversation.

So, I'm the villain
I'm the one who is wrong
Living in spite of others makes me a legion.

So, this is evil?
(I prefer to call it fashion sense)
Yes, I'm the hubris, the vice
cast into the role of foe
by a roll of the dice.

"When I'm Catatonic"
2013: *Taste*

> When it happens
> That's when I take my hands
> off the wheel, shut my eyes
> I like being partially blind.
> That's when I compromise
> I do whatever tickles my tenderloins.
>
> I wish I had dreams worth escaping to
> but I only have when I'm catatonic.
> Sometimes I even wish I could take you there, too.
> You writhe, injured, between my thumb
> and forefinger - I know you.
> There's still so much left I could show you.
>
> Those wiry tones creep
> out of my register
> If they don't feel my revenge
> how on Earth will they ever learn?
> They'll never learn.
>
> We'll circle each other
> in the arena
> snarling and spitting into the dust.
> A playful tackle, a bite at the ear
> we're getting much too into it all.

"Clitoris"
2013: *Facetious Melody*

> Looks like it's just you and me
> this Halloween.
> By now it seems, my stomach
> has settled into the routine of swimming
> in that vast uncertainty.
>
> I'll circle you
> in the arena
> snarling and spitting into the dust.
> A playful tackle, bite at the ear;
> I'm enough for the both of us.
> And among all the turbulent distress,
> I find your...
>
> Intrigue drips between
> the wavelengths' dips and peaks
> ...now that's not something ya often see.
> But you've still got that same old
> gasoline sloshing around in there
> since way back when.
>
> Yes, now I'm quite certain
> my stomach has settled into the routine.

"I Am A Goddamned Bird"
2013: *Facetious Melody*

>
> I wish
> I was using your metaphor
> I am a goddamned bird, it hurts.
> The scars on my back
> where skin has burst
> sewn crudely shut, can't contain
> my worst.
> Bones full of air attempt
> to stretch
> hurts
> in hiding
> bait in breath
> makes me sick every time it gets worse.
> I swell senseless pumping life
> in foreign parts.
> ...
> Voice devolving!
> Hoarse, sickly squelching!
> Idiot animal!
> Can't even speak!
> Pressed in flesh!
> Sewn in meat!
> No sensible grounds!
> Awareness the same.

SUAVITY'S MOUTHPIECE + FUTURE TENANT

present

THE NUANCE EXHIBITION

a celebration of the fine subtleties of Pittsburgh-based artistic music

DISPOSABLE REDHEAD (live electronics) • **IVENFAINT** (new new wave)

SUAVITY'S MOUTHPIECE (anti-pop)   **AND SPECIAL GUEST**

CHRISTIANE D (esque)

SATURDAY, AUGUST 4TH
7PM • $5 ADMISSION
For further information, please visit futuretenant.org

819 penn ave.
pittsburgh, pa
15222

futuretenant.org

SUAVITY'S MOUTHPIECE
PEERLESS SUAVITY

ALBUM RELEASE SHOW

featuring supporting performances by

Nevhar Anhar
PGH AVANT JAZZ

The Spectres
PGH SURF PUNK

Midge Crickett
PGH LIBRARY POP

LIVE AT UNION PROJECT
801 N. NEGLEY AVE • PGH 15206

SEPTEMBER 15
ADMISSION $5

"Peerless Suavity" CDs available for $5

MORE INFO at SMPOP.TK

The Union Project does not endorse the views of organizations, groups or individuals that rent space at the Union Project.

Midge Crickett.

Prayher.

J. Trafford.

L̲IVE AT M̲ODERNFORMATIONS G̲ALLERY

7pm – $5 admission

Saturday, May 16

MORE INFO AT SMPOP.TK

Suavity's Mouthpiece

• • • • • • • •

10th ANNIVERSARY PERFORMANCE
with special guests

DINOSOUL

&

Jess Klein

SATURDAY, HAMBONE'S
AUGUST 11 7PM

For more information please visit smpop.tk

"Support Your Local Library" - new 14-track
SM compilation out Summer on Seer Records.

Greensburg Benefit Party for No More Dysphoria

Friday, October 19 • 6pm • @ DV8 Espresso Bar & Gallery

No More Dysphoria is a non-profit organization helping transgender individuals pay for major aspects of their transition.
nomoredysphoria.com

- FEATURING LIVE MUSIC BY -

LOOSELY DEFINED

SAME MOON

J. TRAFFORD

SCRATCHY BLANKET

ANDREW MUSE

SUAVITY'S MOUTHPIECE

LOOSELY DEFINED

THE PETALS

LIVE AT
BLACK FORGE

Saturday, May 25
$5 // 7pm

Halloway Williams   Sommelier   Hearken   Shamar   Thousandzz of Beez

Sounds for Sisters
A BENEFIT FOR SISTERS PGH

at BLACK FORGE COFFEE II

SAT, JUL 9  7PM $10

ST. PATRICK'S REVENGE

FRIDAY, MARCH 18

Bath Time

Sommelier

God's Green Apples

at
CASEY'S

8PM — 1811 E. CARSON ST - PGH — $10

Sommelier
CANZONI, ILLUMINAZIONE DI FriendlySpinach

Gala Rise & the Uprising
CANZONI, ILLUMINAZIONE DI Lindsey Shaw

Loose Rhetoric
CANZONI, ILLUMINAZIONE DI Steven Haines

Moontown
CANZONI, ILLUMINAZIONE DI Chris Palmer

CODE & CREMATORY
MUSIC + PROJECTION SHOW

SAT, FEB 24 · ROBOTO · 7PM · $5 · MASKS REQUIRED

sommelierband.com

TROLL 2
SOMMELIER
FUNKY LAMP
BROTHAMANS
COLIN & THE
CROWS

Little Giant
wed, april 17 - 7pm - $5
100 ASTEROID WAY, PGH 15210 · SOMMELIERBAND.COM

MUSIC FESTIVAL

SUN, JUNE 2 • 1PM–9PM
ORMSBY AVE CAFE (OUTDOORS)
ALL AGES • $12 ADV • $15 DOS

QUEER ART VENDORS! LIVE MUSIC! PERFORMANCES BY

**LYLYTH • SOMMELIER • ODD ATROCITY
BRYCE BOWYN • SHERRY CD-ROM • CASEY CATONE
RHYTHM OF THE NIGHT FUSION BAND • V.V.ITCH
KING BLUE HERON • K9DIET • KUMANJI JOHNSON**

DJ SET BY **PWUPPY**

FOOD TRUCK!

ALL PROCEEDS BENEFIT

HUGH LANE
@hughlanewellness

TRAFFORD ESTATE & MR. SMALLS PRESENTS

NOW HERE WOLVES

LIVE RECORD RELEASE
FEATURING PERFORMANCES BY

NORMAL CREATURES **SAMURAE** **THE STOLEN STITCHES**

WEDNESDAY, NOVEMBER 13

THE FUNHOUSE AT MR. SMALLS
400 LINCOLN AVE - MILLVALE, PA
DOORS 7PM | $12 ADV | $15 DOOR

WWW.TRAFFORD.ESTATE

"Learn Some Fucking Finesse"
2014: Non-album single

The title of this film is:
The friend who refused to fuck-off
(Let's watch)

A prescience
of this verum dramatis
has already become apparent to me

Be mad; or learn some fucking finesse!
'Relief' represents an incomprehensible unknown.

I don't know why we, as a point of habit
cower at the rain;
I'm gonna make a change, but ONLY
to that

You've just incurred the stinging wrath
of the entire ensemble!
How foolish you must be to misstep

as if you're such a catch!

Be mad; or learn some fucking finesse.
Learn some fucking finesse!

"Good Exercise"
2014: *Peerless Suavity*

>	For one divine moment,
>	it's as if neither Sinatra nor Presley
>	ever died.
>	Then: side-longed into the median.
>
>	This is the slab of metal
>	that makes it work
>	And it is a lifelong longing to explore
>	the grave.
>
>	Your canal caves in
>	and crushes my invader!
>	And, all at once
>	the game beats its
>	dying pulse
>	All I want is jailtime
>	for the rest of my life:
>	It's good exercise.
>
>	And did you ever pity me
>	anytime you turned to see the reliquary
>	Does it matter that this is me?
>	What's vital is that I'm
>	getting good exercise.

"Why Must I Be A Boycrazy Teen?"
2014: *Peerless Suavity*

    He's here, now
    he's on the other floor of the house.
    What will he say when he's seen…?
    I've torn my dress to shreds
    in my spiky hands?

    Will he never forget tonight, well
    I'm sure it's playing out quite differently in his head.
    Talking with my dad, nodding
    through everything he says just
    wants to see his *babe*.

    But - somehow I am no longer
    his babe.

    Certainly! Such sudden silence below
    cannot be right.
    Hollow footsteps on the flight,
    the door creaks in I
    turn rigid tale to see:

    Oh my God…he's even worse than me.

"All Moonlight"
2014: *Peerless Suavity*

> In moonlight,
> your ministrations lie
> just north of the itch
> From this overlook,
> and your blue eyes
> ...*you bitch.*
>
> Coupe creeps forward,
> crypt creeps toward the edge
> of this overlook, and heat
> as soup-steam
> pours
> right off our old Ford.
>
> In our high school,
> we both know I
> could cleanly fit the contours
> of this winsome mold
> But that thing that I become
> ...*well, there's no need to tell*
> *your parents 'bout that.*
>
> From this overlook,
> I'd turn up the radius on the noise

surrounding the space and create stars, I guess.

On my own in our high school, well
I could still cleanly fit the mold, but
How many shrinks could I lie to
in a matter of months?
Together, we're open-facing wounds.
And love is just something to do
for two.

"Atone"
2015: Non-album single

Who knew you'd follow through?
Now, we're stripped to the skin before each other,
and it's your move.
I see hesitation in your iris's bloom, lover
this dance is older than age,
practiced every day by youth.

When our mambo is through,
and the skin and the bone's broken through
Don't you know you've still yet to atone?

The exquisite delight of
three people moving in time
on petals and ready grapes of wrath.

When our pulses are soothed,
and the skin is sheen in vermouth

From my point of view, you've still yet to atone?

Then, all of a sudden when silence comes
over the room
Take your hand from my waist, and
let the needle find the groove.

"Sitcom"
2015: B-side of *Atone*

Snatch sweetest fruit
from the empty air
That's what you do
You'll be thanked for your sins
later, but
you better hope there's a later.
Peel away...

Each step sinking
in clods of loam,
other things wondering
if they are alone.
The pests' whistling wings drone

A decision has been made!
The planets have nothing to do with me
Now rocks pock the dead air,
and no one could consider our life.

Smiling into your flute
do you think you know something?
Well, you'd better watch your step
'cuz you could be next.

In paradise, her eyes
rise to mine,
and the thrill is that of a bow pulled back.
A brassy whine suffuses the room,
and she confines her breaths to my
many measured moods.

It's like bleeding, only it feels *perfect*.

"Chassis"
2016: *Bellows*

>When in age smoketsains - strange patterns
>on your wall: your memories
>grow into your days
>Each mile that you add to the highway
>stretching back lays in a rich stroke of paint.
>
>Morning's sun fills the fire in your lungs
>lit there when you were a kid.
>Worn ink on your skin burns bolder deeper in
>meaning all it ever did.
>Great chords resound through wood and steel unbound
>witness to an old grace found.
>
>You keep all of this
>in your chassis, old smoky bellows
>two symmetrical scars.
>
>The grit in your hair's not going anywhere -
>now salt's got some pepper to share.
>And the virtue of truth - nowhere truer than in you
>held in a sparrows-heart hue.

"Plainclothes"
2017: Non-album single

> In my moment of weakness,
> I suckled at the status quo, hiccuped
> at the lenience,
> no reticence to the flow
> thieving allegiance in the
> hand that feeds us.
> Fish in a barrel,
> flowers in a vase
> In a couple of years I'll be just an
> empty parking space.
> I'll season the wound,
> brick up the bookcase.
>
> Don't I pay for these roads?
> Why is my heart in my throat?
> Aren't I being good?
> Civil saving grace,
> show me how to
> behave like I really should.
>
> Lambs landed in pasture
> only by circumstance
> Never moved faster than when the TV
> showed us how to dance.
> New meat's coming in

where skin's never been.
The cure for what ail's ya's
always de mode
The hair of the dog?
One of two bad sommeliers.
What more do we need?
What more can we take?

Don't I pay for these roads?
Why is my heart in my throat?
Aren't I being good?
Knee-deep
in the wool
anyone can be in control;
it's fool's gold.

"Gin Stinger"
2017: Unreleased

    Snowflakes' velveteen caress
    as teardrops crown her evergreen dress
    and she looks up at the moon and believes
    "Someone must be willing to come back for me."

    Beneath a starry chandelier, praying
    for the mercy of its many years
    Each step shone within the vamp
    of her blocky boots
    in a burn of blue

    Ice bobs in a ballet
    beneath the broth -
    a teardrop spent
    is a part of you lost.

    She looks down at her feet,
    and concedes...
    "Your olive branch doesn't extend to me."

    But there's something in the wisp of the leaves.

"Ronnie the Rhododendron"
2020: Non-album single

    He's peripheral for a reason
    when he's out taking the sunlit breeze in
    If he tells you he loves you, you can believe him
    Honesty must be so freeing.

    He's strong, and he knows
    how he'll take the next blows
    his nose curls into a rose

Just wants to blend in
Didn't ask for no attention
If you were to ask any one of those ancients in Denton:
'He's so far from heaven,
he dismisses divine intention.'
I reckon that that's the consensus
But ask anybody whose word's worth a mention
Ronnie's a rhododendron.

Licorice for lunch
then headed back to bed
He wants a life where he bites off
more than a breath

Black curls fall tight to the saintly head

they part so tame to a knowing hand
What's life but pain
that friends and art can amend
when I get up to meet them?

Just wants to blend in
Didn't ask for no attention
If you were to ask any one of those ancients in Denton:
'He's so far from heaven,
he dismisses divine intention.'
I reckon that that's the consensus
But ask anybody whose word's worth a mention
Ronnie's a rhododendron.

"My Hypocrisy"
2020: Non-album single

    Cloaked in aromas
    my hypocrisy
    bleeds from the nave to the sanctuary
    Me in the present; me in the past;
    and future me - that's the Holy Trinity.

    Trails all through your gauntlet of lights:
    is this what you want out of a disciplined life?
    Perfume or pain?
    It's all the same.

    In my nightmare youth it's what
    got me through
    Now in age it's an all-consuming phage.
    I can set my devotion-like irons in the fire
    When the star shutters a final time.

    I lock my vice wide for
    the feeding of the choir.

    I'm just proving me -
    write about me
    Unequal persuasion - persistent equation.
    And will the strongest people I know, stop crumbling?

Stick to your word raise your heads from the heard.
You hate that I meditate on all the evils
done to me, but then you're floored
when the world gets worse:
String-bean believes!
Better days will come, one can be
forgiven for being that dumb.

In my nightmare youth it's what got me through
Now in age it's an all-consuming phage.
I can set my devotion-like irons in the fire
When the star shutters a final time.

I lock my vice wide for the feeding of the choir.

"Cassingle"
2020: Non-album single

> Let the house be swallowed in its sleep!
> They're blind to see you're
> in-step with the music
> Isn't it wild if just to think
> your problems are all your own making?
>
> Learn to trust new instincts.
> You lift the life out of my lungs
> Steal the song from off my tongue –
> it's as if you need to
> get hurt to get anything done.
>
> You express your languid views decked
> only in two saddle shoes
> But little piggies five through two
> lament the lot they drew.
>
> You're doing your best we
> see the beads of sweat
> You only need the least encouragement
> Burn your light back to the stars
> and we'll believe.

"Don't Express Yourself"
2021: *Don't Express Yourself*

Something's off
this diamond in the rough
A theatre-geek's Greek ideal
arm's-length, head wrong
Possession is aggression
and he's of the mind to get
ground to the rind
That's fine, as far as I'm concerned
They'll live with what they have learned.

The Meanies, a legion, gleaming
Don't express yourself
Those snakey ways borne deep in each
unsmiling face
Summon some grace, meet me halfway.

A meal to the metal
And a call from the sluice
Spew loose from the kettle.

Those first few moment of death
in character - off set
My warbling is marbling
in peopled purposelessness

What could be worse than this?
X walked
so Y could run, but where were they when
you were having your fun?

The Meanies, a legion, gleaming
Don't express yourself
Those snakey ways borne deep in each
unsmiling face
Summon some grace, meet me halfway.

From bow to hull
How I'd love to lose weight in my skull,
and now it can't take much
I am just as afraid as I was on the first day

The Meanies, a legion, gleaming
Don't express yourself
Those snakey ways borne deep in each
unsmiling face
Summon some grace, don't express yourself.

"Idiot"
2021: *Survivalist*

    We fuck things up
    a little more
    with each return
    When we loose our grips
    drop down
    from the branches
    the dumbest sound I've ever heard.
    I'll make no excuse
    for a ruddy youth, to whom
    acting upon a point of view
    is something an idiot would do.
    You boo-hoo, it's still no use
    but if I can outlast
    abject disappointment, so can you.
    Inviting temptation in the desert, so
    show us what you are worth -
    you'll pardon my repeat in the garden,
    an idiot stalls expecting a different result.
    Have you taken your patience pills?
    This whole scheme is nothing new
    Putting your faith in me unconditionally
    is something an idiot would do
    Serotonin syndrome - self-induced
    is something an idiot would do.

"Killing the Au Pair"
2022: Non-album single

>Cigarette?
>Mind if I do?
>Only one song could ever bleed through
>
>A light in the fog!
>And the dashboard goes dark,
>I'm not trying to get you to think that hard
>
>Was I sloughing, hugging?
>Slumped over his creature comforts -
>abetting my shear
>
>You're a vaulted thunder!
>(when it suits your boots)
>I'm so far in the future
>I'm of no use.
>
>Winter is a moment -
>heaven an instrument
>
>I'm a sensitive shit when
>it comes to him, so
>shut-off when I talk
>it *really* burns me to the wick.

"Bug Bomb"
2023: *Bug Bomb*

Call upon me, fleecing the bathers, o, such
impish behavior!...
You're not the first comedian,
I don't think you
know what the fuck you're doing as a human
Let's trade places!
Don't make me set off the bug bomb,
annoying lover
Better take cover.

A gossamer morning,
and I'm brimming with forgiveness
Arras pulled to center, and
I'm splintering inwards
Life could be SO easy
if the brunt could change.

You've had your window, now
it's time to dispose with going slow.
Annoying lover!
...better learn to take cover
Don't make me drop it,
don't make me set off the bug bomb
I take the light back into my mouth,
across the gums and it's gone.

"Blink And You'll Miss Him"
2023: *Bug Bomb*

>Too many years -
>too many years, and still I'm running
>out of years
>You wait for me to
>go to sleep: it won't be long.
>
>By day 2,
>the second dose will start to plume
>in the ardent ruth
>of the black rearview
>How do you
>get all that you want, life's lot
>a lapping font?
>
>Too many moments cut
>too close to the core
>A dogged-survived, both hinds
>tucked inside
>the Quarreler's dance.
>
>I wasn't doing well
>with tongs, a rose from Hell
>still unspooling seams from 2013
>I couldn't stop the gym disappearing
>with you and him in it.

Glinting, minty rock & roll
could never save your soul
No matter your feelings full
at the roll n' bowl.
Wrack yourself on
the loom for penance,
Beauty's breadth is with whom you share it:
You've pressed as much into my chest.

An expanse of scabs:
He, whose lips curl planting
fare at the tilt-a-whirl,
he, who dyed rosebud tips
blows the scent off hyacinths.

"Hip Hop"
2023: *Bug Bomb*

Kai rides
on a tailwind of whimsy, eyedropping
lace-unplanned,
shrapnel understanding
The decadence is SO demanding

Maybe you don't need so much scenery
Fickle sibilance hides your hints

I've washed your bowl
and folded your towel!

There's no one else left on the planet now -
I'm no polymath, you can see the crystals on my breath

In puffed and lasting light,
in marzipan dawn
where all equals parcel on

laziness is a factor

If you're anything like me as a drunk,
there'll be denial of the hand at the cliffside.

HOW DARE HIGH ART FORCE A WEDGE IN
DRIVE US APART?

"Attitude Adjustment"
2024: *Nowhere Wolves*

When I was in charm school,
I dipped my hand into the dish
too deeply, one too many times,
and they had to take me aside.
I got nervous - it'd defeat the purpose.
If you want, I'll abide
I fear, I'll have to be taken aside
I stormed onto shards trying
to be the world's smartest singer
Losing proving ground when they saw
what they didn't like,
grasped me back and took me aside.

www.ingramcontent.com/pod-product-compliance
Lightning Source LLC
LaVergne TN
LVHW012036060526
838201LV00061B/4640